D0344309

NO LONGER PROPERTY OF
SEATTLE PUBLIC LIBRARY

THE ROAD TO DEMOCRACY IN IRAN

THE ROAD TO DEMOCRACY IN IRAN

Akbar Ganji

Foreword by Joshua Cohen and Abbas Milani

A Boston Review Book

THE MIT PRESS Cambridge, Mass. London, England

Copyright © 2008 Massachusetts Institute of Technology

All rights reserved. No part of this book may be reproduced
in any form by any electronic or mechanical means (including
photocopying, recording, or information storage and retrieval)
without permission in writing from the publisher.

MIT Press books may be purchased at special quantity
discounts for business or sales promotional use. For
information, please e-mail special_sales@mitpress.mit.edu or
write to Special Sales Department, The MIT Press,
55 Hayward Street, Cambridge, MA 02142.

This book was set in Adobe Garamond by *Boston Review*
and was printed and bound in the United States of America.

Text design by Joshua J. Friedman.

Library of Congress Cataloging-in-Publication Data
Ganji, Akbar.
  [Essays. English. Selections]
  The road to democracy in Iran / Akbar Ganji ; foreword by
Abbas Milani and Joshua Cohen ; translated by Abbas Milani.
      p.   cm. — (A Boston review book)
  Includes bibliographical references.
  ISBN 978-0-262-07295-3 (hardcover : alk. paper)
  1. Democracy—Iran.   2. Human rights—Iran.   I. Milani,
Abbas.   II. Title.
JQ1789.A15G367   2008
320.955—dc22   2007050401

10   9   8   7   6   5   4   3   2   1

For Masoumeh Shafiee—

*for her solidarity in our common struggle
and her sacrifices for our family*

CONTENTS

Joshua Cohen and Abbas Milani

FOREWORD

OVER THE COURSE OF ITS HUNDRED-YEAR history, the Iranian democratic movement has had a particularly complicated relationship with Shiism—Iran's state religion. That complexity owes in part to competing tendencies within Shiism. One strand has sought to reconcile Islam with modern rationalism, democracy, and the rule of law. The second, powerfully expressed in Ayatollah Khomeini's idea of a rule of the judges, has disparaged democracy and rationalism as modernist diseases and turned Shiism into a project for religious domination of the state.

In each of the three pivotal moments of modern Iranian history—the 1905 Constitutional Revolution, the 1951-53 effort by Dr. Mossadeq to create a nationalist and democratic polity, and the 1979 Islamic revolution—these two competing tendencies played a crucial political role. It is a measure of Akbar Ganji's eventful public life that he has experienced and embraced, adopted and reformed, and finally transcended both. His personal odyssey provides a window on recent Iranian history, and is, at the same time, a potent metaphor for the lives of a whole generation of devout Iranians, invariably from the lower classes, who came of age in the period leading to the revolution, grew disillusioned with the utopian dreams of the revolution, and finally rejected the idea of an Islamic state and the ambition of creating an "Islamic democracy."

Ganji was born in Tehran, in a working-class neighborhood now famous because of the very large number of radical Iranian Islamists who also grew up there. Deeply pious and a staunch supporter of the 1979 Islamic revolution, he joined the Revolutionary Guard at its creation, and eventually served in the Iraq War (1980-88). Ganji was influenced both by Ayatollah Khomeini's charisma, and by Ali Shariati's rationalized, modernized version of Shiism. Shariati, a French-trained sociologist, eclectically mixed Frantz Fanon and Shiism, Marxism and Structuralism to forge Shia theology into a revolutionary political ideology.

In 1982, Ganji was one of a small group of Revolutionary Guard commanders who concluded that Iran could not defeat Iraq. In a still unpublished letter to Ayatollah Khomeini, they described the strategic stalemate, and urged that Iran accept a cease-fire. Khomeini disagreed, and Ganji soon resigned from the Guard. But his break with the regime was not complete. For the next two years, he served as a cultural attaché to the Islamic Republic's embassy in Turkey. He used the opportunity to study and promote Shariati's ideas in Turkey, while also learning from the experience of the Islamic democratic forces that were then emerging in Turkish politics and now rule the country.

As Khomeini's political Shiism created and then prolonged a reign of terror, Ganji felt increasingly alienated from the regime. He turned to journalism and quickly established his reputation as his generation's most successful investigative reporter. Ganji's collection of essays on the financial corruption of the Rafsanjanis, and his revelation about the infamous case of Serial Murders—a project to kill Iranian intellectuals—were national bestsellers. His political philosophy also began to change, leading him finally to the conviction that democracy and respect for human rights were Iran's best hope.

Ganji's insistent defense of human rights and his groundbreaking work as an investigative journalist finally landed him in an Iranian prison where he stayed for more than six years. In protest against the injustice of his treatment, he went on a hunger strike for more than seventy days. His defiance and humility, his fearless defense of human rights, and his insistence on speaking the truth, even at great personal cost, brought him broad international support and, finally, his freedom.

While in prison, Ganji smuggled out a long essay that expressed his new political outlook. This work, called *Republican Manifesto*, represented a sharp departure from his past attempts to find a version of Shiism that could serve as a public philosophy in a modern democracy. In a modern democracy, he concluded, religion cannot serve as a guide to official conduct or as a basis of law and policy. At the same time, Ganji rejected—by personal example and theoretical argument—the clerical and radical-secularist argument that secular politics means the death of religion. Private piety, Ganji argued, can coexist with secular politics: a religious society, whose members are devout, can be a secular polity, in which religion has no special privilege. Indeed, religion thrives under modern conditions only if it limits itself to the private domain, and leaves the public arena of law and policy as a shared space for deliberation founded on our common reason. Borrowing from a wide array of sources—from Rawls and Rorty to Locke and Tocqueville—Ganji has shaped a secular and democratic public philosophy, guided first and foremost by a concern for justice.

The essays collected in *The Road to Democracy* were all initially presented as lectures. Deborah Chasman, co-editor of the *Boston Review*, and Rebecca Tuhus-Dubrow, associate editor, have edited them for length and clarity, while preserving their personal and informal tone. (In a few places, when Ganji was clearly aiming to speak for the Iranian democratic movement, "I" has been changed to "we.") We thank them

for their work, which has made it possible
to publish this important book.

Joshua Cohen and Abbas Milani
December 2007

PROLOGUE

Today, June 29, 2005, is the nineteenth day of my second hunger strike. I first went on a hunger strike for eleven days in late May. In total, over the course of thirty days of fasting, my body weight has plummeted from 77 kilograms to 58 kilograms.

I have been sent to solitary confinement in Evin Prison. I have been denied telephone communications, visitors, newspapers, and walks in the open air.

Authoritarian systems turn lying from a vice to a virtue. In Iran liars claim: we have no political prisoners and no solitary cells, there are no hunger strikes in our prisons, our prisons are like hotels. This Orwellian use of language does not change reality. Prison means deprivation of freedom, and a political prisoner is one who is imprisoned for expressing dissenting views. In recent years, as all global human rights organizations have confirmed, Iran has jailed hundreds of dissidents.

Tehran's prosecutor, Saeed Mortazavi, exemplifies the Iranian regime's disregard for the truth. One day, he claims that Ganji has been sent to a solitary cell for his hunger strike. Another day he announces that Ganji is in solitary confinement to learn a lesson and he will stay there until he learns it. Yet in his last statement he says, "Since Ganji has medical problems, doctors have recommended that he stay in a quiet environment away from disturbance." Liars forget their previous lies and fabricate new ones. They have forgotten that the head of Tehran's Justice Department, Abbasali Alizadeh, claimed a month ago that Ganji was not sick. Now they say that doctors have diagnosed him with respiratory problems. Have doctors recommended that I be denied telephone communication, visitors, newspapers, and fresh air? Did they order prison officials to put a drug dealer, sentenced to fifteen years in jail, in my cell at 12:20 am on June 17 to finish me off? (They had taken that drug dealer the day before to Saeed Mortazavi, who had briefed him on what he had to do that night. The person who had accompanied him from Mortazavi's office to my cell was telling the wardens that, if it had been up to him, he would have tossed my dead body on the floor himself. Of course I had heard that they intended to kill me; and as they tried to bring the drug dealer into my cell, I called out loudly so that other prisoners would know that they were trying to kill me. I had witnesses and they left me alone in my cell.)

Let it be known that if learning my lesson means denouncing my views, I will never learn my lesson; that all my writings are the result of deliberation and research. Let it be known that Akbar Ganji will not cease his hunger strike until he achieves his goal of letting the world know that there is a committed democracy movement in Iran. Forcing repentance letters on prisoners is the method of Stalin's interrogators, inherited by Iranian Stalinists.

Today my broken face is the true face of the system in the Islamic Republic of Iran. My ravaged body exposes the regime's oppressiveness. Anyone who sees me now asks in surprise, "Are you Akbar Ganji?

What have they done to you?"

They hide this body from the public to hide the reality of the Islamic Republic. They do not allow reporters to take my picture.

As I have said before, if I die in prison, it is on the orders of Mr. Khamenei, the Supreme Leader, from whom Mortazavi gets his orders. I have opposed the undemocratic rule of Mr. Khamenei, who is unelected and unaccountable to the people. I have said that expressing this opinion would provoke Mr. Khamenei's quick and harsh reaction. My incarceration has proved me right. He does not tolerate any personal criticism. Mehdi Karroubi, Mustafa Moeen and Ali Akbar Hashemi Rafsanjani, reformist candidates with some popular support, all tasted Mr. Khamenei's "religious democracy" in the last election. The widespread and organized interference of the Revolutionary Guards Corps and Basij militia in the election drew outcry even from the conservative Ali Larijani's campaign staff and from Mohsen Rezaei. Mortazavi has said to my wife: "What will happen if Ganji dies? Dozens die every day in prisons; Ganji will be just one of them." These are Mr. Khamenei's words uttered through Mortazavi's lips. I may die, but the demands for freedom, democracy, and justice will continue to live.

> *Happy it is when the touchstone of*
> *experience cometh in play*
> *So are left disgraced those who conceal*
> *impure alloy.*
> —Hafez, 14th-century Persian poet

Akbar Ganji
June 29, 2005

THE ROAD TO
DEMOCRACY
IN IRAN

1

ONE OF THE MOST PRESSING PROBLEMS of our time is the widespread violation of human rights, the reduction of human beings to mere tools. This crassly instrumental view has aroused the opposition of the world community. Yet human rights violators often deny the existence of universal human rights. Some claim we have local or regional human rights (Asian, African, European, American); others refer to cultural human rights (Islamic, Christian,

Jewish, Buddhist, Confucianist); and a third group believes in human rights specific to different civilizations (Western, Eastern). Certain governments, as well as some postmodernists, communitarians, and fundamentalists, have declared their opposition to the concept of universal human rights. Countries including Singapore, Malaysia, Taiwan, and China drafted a resolution in 1992, taking issue with the universality of human rights, and defending the local values of Eastern cultures as emanating from the Confucian doctrine. Here I want to raise two important questions. First, we must ask why there is only one set of human rights. Second, we ask why we must fight for their realization.

The idea of universal human rights is founded on the belief that human beings, in spite of some large differences, share a common human essence. Is this really true?

Our reason for believing it is not a priori or rational. Contrary to Aristotle, we do not claim that every human being has a common and unchanging essence, while only attributes are plural and changing. According to Aristotelian essentialists, for example, if a gallon of water undergoes changes, freezing and melting and evaporating, it will nonetheless remain water and will have the same essence as water anywhere in the world. This proposition implies that in spite of their many physical, psychological, sociological, and historical differences, humans too all share the same essence, which has remained constant throughout history.

Our position is different. We are not essentialists. We do believe, however, that the entire population of the world today is capable of suffering. This contention derives from a posteriori and empirical evidence. We know that a common set of acts will cause all six billion of us physical and psychological pain. Has there ever been a time when human beings did not suffer from anxiety and fear, anguish and despair, injustice and oppression?

The common experience of pain is thus the foundation for human rights. We believe that any human being who has the capacity to suffer is entitled to certain rights. (Of course, if there are people who because of mental disorders have different thresholds of pain and suffering, their human rights must be as fully respected as those of any healthy man or woman.) Supporters of universal rights, including signatories to the International Declaration of Human

Rights, believe that human beings suffer from common sources, and that we must find ways to spare people these experiences. But we do not believe that those rights are fixed; they are not limited to those specified in the Declaration of Human Rights. The concept of human rights remains open to change: new rights might develop, or old rights might lose their relevance. This mutability has two sources. As humans gain more knowledge about their condition, their self-perception evolves and expands. New understanding of causes of suffering may emerge, and thus require new rights. In addition, as life becomes more developed and more complex, new problems arise. Will today's environmental problems create hitherto unknown causes of pain and suffering, and thus require the establishment of new rights? It is also possible that new inventions or the obsolescence of outdated systems will render some human rights irrelevant.

Yet while the list of human rights is subject to change, the list at any given time applies to the whole of humanity, regardless of civilization or culture, faith or ethnicity, race or nationality. We do not agree with some postmodernists and communitarians, who grant such overwhelming power to historical, geographical, and cultural context that they render unity impossible. We are not relativists.

Only conflicts between rights, in extreme situations, can mitigate human rights. It is possible that members of a society, when faced with a conflict between Right A and Right B, will prefer Right A, while the people of another society will choose Right B. Both societies respect both rights, but in the realm of reality, they must subordinate one to the other. For example, when there is relative security, citizens do not allow the police to randomly intercept documents or to conduct bodily searches on a mere suspicion. But when the society's sense of security is threatened, the citizenry might grant the police these rights. On this point, however, we need to be very clear. It is the society itself, not its rulers, that can make the decision to temporarily temper some rights. No government or authority may suspend rights secretly or without the direct approval of the people themselves. Any suspension of rights must also be clearly and unambiguously limited to short duration. And we must always be conscious that those who do not want to respect human rights can use emergencies to their advantage. History is full of such examples.

In addition, acknowledging that under certain circumstances not all human rights can be realized does not undermine their universality. Ours is essentially a utilitarian point of view. We are not deontologists who believe that certain acts, regardless of their consequences, are good, and certain others, regardless of their results, are bad. For us, what matters in judging an act is its result. Nor are we conservative traditionalists who insist on fidelity to the mores of the past, in spite of the fundamentally different present reality. For example, the belief in the economic necessity of large families has given way, in modern societies, to the current belief in family planning. We do not believe that if a certain deed was deemed wrong in the past, we too must consider it wrong. We pay attention to the effects of human acts under new conditions. That is why we promote reform and oppose the conservative forces in Iran.

Our utilitarianism is not of the positive or classic type associated with Jeremy Bentham; instead it is similar to the negative utilitarianism advocated by Karl Popper. We do not focus on affording the maximum pleasure or utility to the maximum number of people. Rather, we humbly suggest that our goal should be the greatest reduction of pain and suffering for the largest number of people. And we are referring to the kind of experience the people themselves consider painful, rather than those declared to be painful by ideologies and doctrines. We must bear in mind that in their attempt to take societies to a utopian future, free from any suffering, radical social and political projects tend to inflict great suffering on living individuals.

We believe further that human rights have a hierarchy, and at the top stand the rights to well-being and to autonomy. In a sense, we consider all other rights to derive from these two. By well-being I mean the right of individuals to be free of physical and psychological anguish, and by autonomy I mean the right to shape their own fate. If individuals feel free of suffering but know that external forces, not they themselves, are responsible for this condition, then it matters little how prosperous and painless their lives ostensibly are; these individuals will still suffer. Who among us does not want to be the architect of our own fate? The principle of autonomy dictates that individuals must each live according to their own vision: the same principle that mystics, existentialist philosophers and humanist psychologists have called the principle of an authentic life.

An authentic life is in fact an autonomous life wherein conformity, public opinion, fads, traditions, and prejudices have no role. (Of course, the principle of autonomy is not a license for an individual to ignore or impede the rights of another individual.)

The principle of authenticity, or autonomy, leads directly to the principle of pluralism. It is self-evident that when all individuals live only according to their own consciences, we will be faced with a plurality of lifestyles. We embrace this diversity and consider it to be in the interest of individuals as well as communities.

This, then, is our position on universal human rights, and it can be summarized in one simple phrase: "Inflict the least pain and suffering." But human rights will not be achieved through academic polemics. Achieving them will require sacrifices from humanists, social reformers, and intellectuals; these torments are our next subject.

Historical experience shows that in every society, the recognition of human rights has required a long and tortuous struggle.

Why?

For us many of the articles of the Declaration of Human Rights are so self-evidently true that we think they need not be proved. But when we remember that the declaration is a historical document, the result of modern thought, we then understand why it has opponents. Belief in this document requires belief in rationalism, in the essential equality of human beings, and in individualism. The notion of human rights depends on the belief in the value of the individual and of the authentic life; it challenges mythical, superstitious, and unscientific views. Even today opponents of human rights are not limited to despotic rulers. We can even find theorists who question the philosophical foundations of the declaration (namely, the faith in the power of human rationality to solve problems of earthly living). Others point to deficiencies in certain articles of this declaration.

If every individual recognized the rights of the Other, opposition to human rights would vanish. Both the declaration and its philosophical underpinnings are based on the notion of tolerance, and on the belief that no one has a monopoly on the truth. We believe that collective wisdom, dialogue, and a collaborative search for the truth will always result in better, more complete solutions than an individual search.

But we are far from this reality. The desirable elements of our existence—namely power, wealth, knowledge, and status—are scarce. Not only in politics, but at every level of social life, even within families, power is concentrated among a small minority. We have not yet been able to create institutions based on collective decision-making. The powerful, particularly in the political arena, have proved unwilling to share their power with others. Only after a prolonged, costly, and in most cases bloody struggle have they granted some authority to individuals or groups who represent the majority of society. For dictators, a despotic government is a sweet thing; there is no reason for them to relinquish it freely. The struggle for human rights has always been spearheaded by the lower classes of society, with the assistance of the more educated, idealistic elements in that society.

The same argument applies in the case of social wealth. Inequality in social status is the result of economic inequality. Depending on our role in the production of wealth, we have a corresponding place in the social hierarchy. Democratizing the process of work and production also requires a long struggle and cannot take place unless people come to believe in their political and social equality.

Marx famously argued that, in class-based societies, formal political and legal equality (afforded to the citizens at the level of the superstructure) contradicts the economic inequality that invariably defines these societies. Those who believed that critique have now come to accept that in order to reduce inequality in society, and in order to achieve individual rights, those formal equalities of the superstructure are essential. Still, we must remember that such formal equality is not the ultimate goal; it is only the first step. The democratization of social institutions is crucial and implies the democratization of knowledge. Moreover, this principle ensues from the very nature of modern technological change. Today's modes of communication have provided the majority of people with some access to knowledge. Modernization invariably fosters new ideas. Modern technology enables the exchange of these ideas.

With the technological and informational revolution, with new means of communication and new sources of news, people have become more aware of conditions in other nations and of disparities in quality of life. People who live in traditional societies, that is, societies with undemocratic governments, can easily witness the lives of people in democratic societies. As a result, the struggle for human rights and for higher standards of living takes root and draws the democratic participation of the people. Such a sequence, one could argue, is a new kind of historical determinism.

There is also a moral principle here. With human rights comes the recognition of injustice in everyday life. I witness that other people's rights are being trampled upon; it becomes evident to me that if I do not take action to help achieve the rights of this Other, I will become alienated from my own human essence. The rights of the Other are complementary to my own rights. I must fight for the rights of those who have no right to speak, no right to live as they wish, those who are humiliated, and those who are deemed second-class citizens.

We can thus see that if the struggle for human rights is intertwined with the democratic struggle, then genuine social progress is possible.

Some in Iran in recent years have claimed that in the age of modernity there is a division of labor, and that intellectuals should not pay the price for what should be the people's own responsibility, or the responsibility of civic institutions that defend human rights. Yet we cannot, as some intellectuals do, rely on concepts and institutions to absolve ourselves of moral responsibilities. Intellectuals must always strive to lessen other people's pain, even though they suffer on this path. And they must live in a way that prepares them to tolerate and survive the pain of insult, exile, imprisonment, and even torture.

But what do these words mean for the current reality in Iran? First of all, the same reasons that have compelled people to fight for human rights throughout history compel Iranian dissidents to struggle for human rights in Iran. We strongly oppose the current laws and policies in Iran, because they do not recognize freedom of thought, freedom of expression, or freedom of religion and assembly. We oppose them because they still sanction the death penalty for an infidel; because they imprison dissidents and those who live differently; because in the last eight years, they have closed more than a hundred magazines and newspapers. We oppose them because according to their version of Islamic law, they have allowed individuals to kill others deemed *mahdour-al dam*, or deserving of death. We oppose them because they have denied the citizens of Iran the right to determine their own fate. They deny the people the right to replace the current rulers in a peaceful manner. They have blocked all democratic methods of reform, and they have deprived our women of many of their civic and political rights.

Declaring these positions is risky. It could easily land me in prison for a third time. But when one believes that one's actions are morally justified, and when one knows that international organizations, as well as thinkers and activists around the world, stand ready to offer spiritual support, then there is no fear. If these goals of democracy and human rights are valuable to us, we must struggle to achieve them.

2

IN IRAN TODAY THERE IS A MOVEMENT TO foster democratic change in the country's political and social system. This collective effort consists of a number of groups, without leaders or hierarchies. The movement is democratic, because we believe that unless we ourselves abide by democratic ideals and practices, we will never succeed in bringing democracy to society at large. Furthermore, our movement advocates reformist change rather than revolution. It does not foment rebellion, nor does it support military action from inside or outside the country. We do not believe that historic change occurs in leaps. As a reformist democratic movement, intended specifically for Iran, it has certain unique characteristics, which I will attempt to outline here.

We believe that the cost of a revolution exceeds its benefits. Swift and radical change must be merely physical and material, rather than psychological or cultural, simply because the latter kind are by their nature slow and gradual. Moreover, physical and material change invariably begets the use of force, and innocent bystanders are thus victimized. Such violence lacks moral justification. We must never sacrifice a group, no matter how small, for the sake of another group, no matter how large. Furthermore, violence and force can never win hearts and minds, and are in fact more likely to breed hostility. In the wake of revolutionary violence many people would remain at best indifferent to the ideals and institutions of a new government and, indeed, would likely feel alienated from it.

Revolutions are based on a false premise, which we might call "political essentialism." This theory posits that a society's political regime is the primary source of all problems, and that societal improvement entails first and foremost the overthrow of the political system. But if politics causes all problems, why then don't these problems disappear when the ancient regime is overthrown? The violence used by victorious revolutionaries is at least partially the result of anger at the realization that their theory was wrong.

By contrast, cultural essentialism suggests that the main source of a society's problems is its culture. By culture I mean the collection of a society's beliefs, emotions, desires, and rituals, as well as its common intellectual, behavioral, and psychological models. Unless the unhealthy cultural indices of a society are ameliorated, even dramatic upheaval in social and political institutions will be useless. The part of the population that retains the original culture will sooner or later change the new political system back to the status quo, and the same miseries and signs of underdevelopment will once again prevail.

Changing people's attitudes is easily one of the slowest human processes. Threats, coercion, or violence cannot create belief; nor can a belief be washed away from minds with these tactics. For this reason, the democratic reform movement has come to accept that cultural changes are a primary goal. But culture has deep roots.

Much of what needs to change in Iranian culture relates to the superstition, dogmatism, conformism, and prejudice that have permeated our society, particularly in the Shia seminaries. Rejecting these aspects of the dominant religious culture in no way implies rejecting religion. Indeed, a considerable number of democratic reformist activists in Iran hold deep religious beliefs. But without reform of these aspects of religious culture in Iran, democratic change will fail.

We must not resign ourselves to the argument that Islam and Shiism are in their essence inimical to reforms, religious or otherwise. It is possible to remain a Muslim and a Shia and to believe wholeheartedly in the reforms advocated by the democratic movement. The nature of our movement requires that we attract the widest possible array of people, regardless of their beliefs; the arena for the democratic struggle must be open to all.

Yet a considerable contingent of Iran's current clergy cannot accept the cultural reforms we advocate. After all, the people's ignorance and superstitions bolster the clergy's power and reinforce their conservatism. Two other factors have redoubled the clergy's opposition to democracy: the considerable number of them who have ascended to political power, and the rise of fundamentalist tendencies among the clergy.

Fundamentalist readings of Islam and Shiism are inimical to the democratic process. Fundamentalism disdains the rational mind. It limits religion almost entirely to Islamic jurisprudence (*fegh*), viewing its laws as intractable and infallible. It embraces the use of violence in establishing a society ruled by divine law, Shari'ah. According to the fundamentalist ideology, religion and the clergy must intercede in every aspect of social life. This ideology also opposes Western culture; religious and political pluralism are anathema to fundamentalists. The reform movement must make every effort to expose the shallow and wanton nature of fundamentalism.

As the religious wing of the reform movement emphasizes, however, democratic evolution is altogether compatible with the modernist reading of Islam. Modernist Islam affords great value to reason. Moreover, it considers piety to consist of living according to a morality that is universal, humanist, and sensitive to pain and suffering. It opposes the creation of a state based on Shari'ah and *fegh*. Indeed, it considers the separation of religion and politics desirable and necessary. Modernist Islam believes in religious and political pluralism, and it is not wholly averse to Western culture, though it might offer some criticism of it. Finally, modernist Islam accepts that we, not foreigners, are responsible for our problems.

The reform movement embraces universal rules, universal morality, and universal human rights. While we disagree about some of the elements of these concepts, we will rely on them alone in resolving the movement's inner tensions and addressing Iran's problems. Thus, it can be said that our movement is modern, and not pre- or postmodern; it subordinates even its own tradition to universal concepts and it repudiates postmodern analysis, especially subjecting morality and human rights to relativism.

Reform can be classified as democratic only when it reduces prejudices and unjust privileges. So it is our goal in Iran to revoke the privileges that rulers have taken for themselves and their relatives. The current regime is founded on a fundamental prejudice that places the *fagih*, or the advisory council of clerics, in the role of a guardian (*Velayat*) and in turn casts the people as ignorant minors. This structural inequity has in turn given rise to other prejudices, most saliently the prejudice against women. Abolishing the existing gender apartheid in Iran is thus a crucial task for the democratic reform movement.

Leveling hierarchies is related to the demand for separation of religion and politics. Ending discrimination by clergy against non-clergy, and by the "insiders" against the "outsiders" (*Khodi* and *Gayre*

Khodi), will not alone suffice to establish justice in Iran. But it is the first step in that direction. We cannot end cultural prejudice—against classes, women, ethnicities, and styles of living—unless we eliminate the structural prejudice of the system. Again this task requires the advent of secularism in the political system.

In Iran democratic reformism aims for republicanism. Special rights are commensurate neither with reason nor with the lessons of history; they lead to despotism. Republicanism, conversely, is based on equality and transparency in political matters. The principle of equality demands that no position can by special right belong to any person or group or family. In a republic all political offices are held on a rotating basis, and the law reigns supreme. All matters pertaining to the republic must be handled by the people. A republican system has no mystery requiring the rule of a special profession. Turning politics into a kind of ritual mastered only by the select few is the origin of corruption in the body politic.

If the public domain is transparent, not only democracy, but peace—peace at home, and peace between nations—becomes possible. Given the exigencies of our time, the special role of Iran in the global context today, and the lessons we have learned from history, we must put peace as both a goal and principle of democratic reform.

Opposing the struggle against the spread of the atomic arsenal in the region is part of our campaign for peace with nature. We call on the conscience and the will of the people everywhere to fight against the destruction of our ecosystem; the environmental movement is in complete solidarity with the peace movement. But we also must make peace an essential principle in our method. Peace, freedom, and ending all forms of prejudice are intertwined to the core.

Peace, though, in no way means submission to the status quo. On the contrary, it requires an incessant critique of our regime's violent nature. Activist advocacy of peace means rejecting all laws that have a coercive nature. The difference between the revolutionary activism of Iran's past and our movement is that the former had no compunction about using the tactics of its rival, but we will promote our cause with civil disobedience. We will stand up peacefully against our coercive and violent regime and act shoulder to shoulder with the people, under the watchful eyes of the entire republic. Only movements that remain dedicated to peace, freedom, and ending prejudice at every stage of their evolution can achieve victory and remain righteous.

We are aware that today the fundamentalism and adventurism of Iran's regime is creating tensions in Iran's relationship with the world. It may lead Iran to the brink of catastrophe, to economic embargo and global isolation and even to war. We are also aware that war against the regime by external forces might be a cover for expansionist designs on the region: that powerful nations might use their campaign to inflict all manner of injustice on the Iranian people, and paint an inaccurate image of us for the world. Therefore, we do not welcome military intervention from the West.

As long as clerical despotism continues, Iran will face two unsavory options: confrontation with the world or submission to the global powers. In both cases the interests of Iranians will be compromised. Democratic reformism in Iran needs to develop an active foreign policy. We republicans advocate negotiations with the U.S. And the movement must show the world the progressive and peaceful nature of the Iranian society. We must make it clear that we are against war, against foreign intervention in Iran, and against solutions imposed by outsiders. At the same time, we must also make clear that we oppose any deal with the regime that undermines the Iranian people's interest in their struggle for freedom and human rights. If our position gains strength, the danger of war diminishes.

But ours is a difficult task, even with full cooperation among groups sharing the same ideals. The social fabric in Iran has been divided by tradition and modernity, by the clergy, and by historical tensions between different groups and political movements. We must for now set aside the hope that we can arrive at consensus in analyzing the failures of our last few decades. Rather, we must cooperate in developing plans and programs based on our goals. Surely insightful historical analysis is valuable, but creating solidarity and offering mutual assistance is far more important. The more we look to the future with optimism and hope, the less heavily will the past weigh upon us.

Criticizing a preoccupation with the past does not mean that we must forget it. The powerful bear special responsibility for explaining past events, particularly those that ended in bloodshed. But only in an atmosphere defined by justice, morality, and liberty can the effort to understand the past truly succeed. Revenge and rancor make understanding impossible. The reformist democratic movement in Iran must emphasize that under no circumstances will its members resort to the gallows or force people into exile. We believe in accountability, but our first priority is peace. We hope that the Iranian democratic movement will be so grounded in peace and forgiveness that the weight of moral criticism will be deemed heavier than any other punishment.

To end the corruption of the current rentier state in Iran and to combat the culture of malignity, mendacity, and corruption, we need moral courage, and the kind of goodwill that can fill the air. Our future democratic evolution must be first and foremost a change in our vision and behavior. We must dedicate ourselves to speaking the truth and persevering. We must not be timid or small-minded, even when we are weak. At every step we must think of moral victory. We can create a new psychology, leading to activism on a grand social scale. And only thus can we change the fight for freedom from a desperate fantasy to a lively, hopeful, and creative struggle.

3

Iran's political-legal system is founded on apartheid, on unjust and untenable discrimination among members of society. Social opportunities and privileges are not distributed on the basis of merit, but according to such indefensible criteria as race, religion, and allegiance to the political regime. While some are deprived of certain basic human rights and the chance to benefit from their talents and efforts, others are afforded "special rights." They benefit handsomely from coveted social opportunities and privileges. One of the most glaring fault lines of this apartheid system is gender. In Iran women suffer every injustice and deprivation endured by Iranian men, and gender injustice as well.

Unfortunately gender apartheid has not drawn as much outrage around the world as racial apartheid has. The international community was rightly united in its opposition to the regime in South Africa that denied blacks equal rights with whites, and it rose up to topple that system. But it has voiced little opposition to many societies in which the rights of women are systematically trampled upon. Under the guise of cultural pluralism, or respect for religious freedom, some clerical leaders have even rationalized gender apartheid.

In Iran those in power justify gender apartheid with religious arguments and claim divine origins for it. They accuse internal critics of violating divine edicts, and through such intimidation they hope to silence defenders of women's rights. With this strategy their own history of passing misogynist laws is cast as a defense of religion and Shari'ah. And because this strategy gains them support from ostensibly apolitical traditionalist religious forces, the regime can use the gender issue to consolidate its political power. That is why every time there is a crisis in Iranian society the regime increases pressure on women and anyone who champions their cause.

Equality should be the foundation of democracy. As a result, equality between men and women must be considered a cardinal element of a democratic system. For this reason fighting discrimination against women has a special place in the Iranian democratic movement. Here I hope to show the areas in which women's rights have been denied on the basis of Shari'ah, and also to address the questions: do the laws that discriminate against women in fact have divine origins, and is rejecting them tantamount to renouncing Islam itself?

It is important first to clarify the term "discrimination against women." According to the UN Convention on the Elimination of All Forms of Discrimination against Women, adopted by the UN General Assembly in 1979, discrimination against women is "any distinction, exclusion or restriction made on the basis of sex which has the effect or purpose of impairing or nullifying the recognition, enjoyment or exercise by women, irrespective of their marital status, on a basis of equality of men and women, of human rights and funda-mental freedoms in the political, econom-

ic, social, cultural, civil or any other field."
One hundred and eighty-five countries are
signatories to this convention, including
all of Iran's neighbors, but Iran is not.

In Iran today, any discussion of laws
that oppress women is dangerous. It can
bring about a prison sentence or even cost
one's life. Religious traditionalists who
support these laws might construe any
such criticism as hubris or an attack on
the prophet. Some clergy have declared
that such critiques imply a rejection of divine edicts, and the more radical followers
of these clerics take such declarations as a
license to kill the critics. Indeed, according
to the criminal laws of the Islamic Republic
of Iran, if someone murders me on the suspicion that I have committed heresy, the
murderer will not receive any punishment
if he proves my heresy in court.

Nonetheless, at the end of this essay I will offer my views on what should be done in the realms of politics, society, and culture to fight the widespread abrogation of women's rights in Iran. Here are some of the most important arenas in which the rights of women are disregarded in the name of religion.

Health and the value of life. Statistics show that Iranian women suffer more than men from hunger and malnutrition, and they have less access to health care. In traditional families boys enjoy more privileges than girls in the realms of medical care, sports, and nutrition; as a result they have better general health. This inequality flows from the cultural attitude—with roots in Shari'ah—that values the life of a man more than the life of a woman. According to Shari'ah the blood money for a man is twice that for a woman. Assume, for example, that an illiterate criminal rapes and brutally murders a woman who is a scholar and a university professor. If the woman's family kills the murderer in retribution (which is allowed by Shari'ah), they must pay the man's family a sum equal to the blood money stipulated in the law for the woman's murder (i.e. the blood money for a man's life, minus that for a woman's), while the man's family pays nothing.

Sanctity of the body. Women's rights to the sanctity of their bodies are freely violated in Iran. Women are, on a large scale, victims of rape, coerced sexual relations with their husbands, domestic violence, and all manner of insults and sexual violations in the public domain. Again Iran's traditional religious culture paves the way for this injustice. One of the obsessions of

Shari'ah is to exercise control over women's bodies. According to traditional religious values, a good woman is chaste. A woman whose behavior deviates from an ideal image of chastity is labeled "unchaste" and men are no longer required to respect her. For example, according to the culture promoted by the rulers in Iran, a woman who is *bad hejab*—who does not wear the clothing approved by the regime—is said to invite men to abuse her sexually. And if she is assaulted the perpetrator easily escapes legal punishment.

The sanctity of women's bodies is also violated regularly in their own homes. According to the traditional interpretation of Islam, a man has the right to physically punish an "unruly" wife. Only if her injuries are excessive can the law, under some circumstances, allow the woman to file for divorce; physical abuse alone is not sufficient grounds for divorce or legal action. Related is the problem of rape in married life. According to the traditional reading, a woman must always comply with her husband's sexual demands. If she refuses, the man has the right to force her into compliance. Underlying the law is the notion that a woman's body is not hers, and that she has no right to make decisions about it on her own. Unfortunately, the concept of rape within marriage is either defended or altogether absent from Iran's cultural and legal discourse. The law can even punish a woman for resisting. There are harsh punishments for rapists who are not married to the victim, but the reasoning is concerned with protecting the husband's property. In short, the law defends not the sanctity of women's bodies, but the rights of men who own them.

The most visible injustices are the humiliating physical punishments meted out to women who have broken the law or are convicted of crimes. For example, the punishment for a woman who engages in an extramarital sexual act is whipping or stoning. According to the law these punishments must be carried out in public.

Dress. Freedom to choose one's own dress is an individual's prerogative. No authority, and certainly not the state, has the right to coerce a certain style of dress on its citizens. Iranian women have long been deprived of this freedom. In modern Iranian history, for example, Reza Shah forced women to take off their head-covers, and subsequently the Islamic Republic forced them to wear head-covers again.

Work outside the home. One of the most important freedoms is the ability to safely seek employment outside the home, to choose one's work, to find employment without discrimination, and to receive fair pay. But Iranian women who work outside their homes must first gain the right to leave home when they wish. According to Shari'ah, a woman can leave the house only if she has the permission of her father or her husband. The husband can easily withhold this permission. In addition, the current legal and political system in the country has strictly forbidden women to hold certain jobs. They cannot become judges, or the president, or the spiritual leaders. It is common practice in the Islamic Republic to bar women from many top governmental posts, including ministerial appointments, the Council of Experts, and the Guardian Council. Excluding women from the centers of power has curtailed their ability to bring about changes in their social condition. Traditionalist Islamic theorists, as well as regime apologists, claim that these restrictions reflect women's natural limitations, that due to their emotional and sensual nature, women are unfit for managerial and leadership positions that require the application of reason and logic.

Mobility and free assembly. If a woman is not entitled to leave her home to work without her husband's permission, neither can she leave it to buy groceries or visit her parents. In many Islamic countries, including Iran, women cannot leave the country without the written permission of their husbands. Needless to say, limiting women's mobility implies, by extension, restricting their right to assembly, particularly for the purpose of political protest.

Free expression and political participation. In a despotic society (such as one based on racial apartheid), even men are deprived of the rights to free expression and political participation, but religion imposes especially strict limits on women in this area. Again, religion's role in limiting women's mobility is likely to limit their free expression and political participation. Another contributing factor is the relatively high rate of illiteracy due to religiously grounded cultural attitudes.

The right of citizenship and the right to transfer it to children. According to the UN convention, the right of citizenship must be transferable to a child equally through the mother and the father. Iranian law allows no independent right of citizenship for women. A child born to an Iranian mother and an Afghan father, for example, is not considered a citizen of Iran and cannot receive an Iranian identity card.

Marriage and family. Family law is the arena where women's rights are most trampled upon in the name of religion. Religious rules as well as traditional culture largely deny women the right to choose their husbands. Most often, men choose their mates, and, particularly in non-urban areas, girls must follow the wishes of their fathers; only a father's permission makes a marriage acceptable in both civil law and Shari'ah. In family life, most crucial decisions about children are made by the father. If the marriage proves unhappy, only the man may file for divorce. Women can ask for divorce only if they can submit to the court special evidence of, say, a husband's impotence or unwillingness to perform his conjugal duties, or desertion. But most often preparing such evidence is impossible. After divorce, the father is invariably granted custody of the children. Another particularly demeaning reality for women is the practice of polygamy. Current laws recognize not only men's right to polygamy but also their right to enter numerous temporary marriages (*sighe*).

Birth control. Fortunately, contraception is legal in Iran today and clinics provide means of preventing unwanted pregnancies as well as family planning programs. But only the pressures of a population explosion led the government to urge theologians to endorse contraception or at least stop publicly opposing it. Bearing fewer children not only improves the health of women, but also fosters better conditions for them to develop and improve their lives. Yet the question of abortion remains a highly sensitive issue in Iranian society. Fatwas issued by many clerics ban abortion, regardless of whether they view the fetus as having a soul. And abortion is legally banned except in extraordinary circumstances. But what is most striking about the clerical debate is the stark absence of any reference to women's right to their own bodies. For Iranian clerics, women do not have such rights, so they are unable to make independent decisions about their bodies, including the decision to terminate a pregnancy.

Education. While women's access to education in Iranian society has improved, considerable obstacles remain. Women's entry into certain fields is either entirely barred or severely limited. In many small towns young girls are denied the chance to study at a major university, since all such universities are in big cities and traditional religious families will simply not allow their young daughters to live in the city unsupervised. Even after graduation, women have a far more difficult time entering the job market and finding suitable jobs in the areas of their expertise.

Is criticizing laws that deny women's rights tantamount to rejecting religion and violating divine edicts? For many people of faith the answer is no. Let me explain.

First, theologians share no consensus on the meaning of many edicts. Even among traditionalist theologians we can find fatwas that contradict some discriminatory laws. In matters under contention, the pious can simply follow the rulings of theologians who have shown more sensitivity to issues of gender justice.

Second, theologians divide the entire collection of religious edicts into two categories: those dealing with prayer (*ebadat*), and those dealing with contracts. The first category covers the relations between individuals and God, such as the laws on daily prayers and fasting. The second category covers social relations between individuals. Laws relating to women fall for the most part in the latter category. Abu Hamid Mohammad al-Ghazali, one of the most eminent theologians in the history of Islam, has suggested that religious laws (particularly those concerning contracts) are not part of religious learning. In his opinion, piety must be defined in ethical and spiritual terms, and not through religious laws (*kalam*).

Similarly, some Shia theologians have argued that doubting or rejecting religious rules is not in itself apostasy. For example, Ayatollah Khomeini, the founder of the Islamic Republic, has written clearly on the subject in one of his books:

> What is essential is Islam, and its acceptance makes a person a Muslim, is the principle of God's existence and of his unity, the prophetic principle, and maybe belief in the day of reckoning. The rest are Islamic rules and they have no relation to the principle of belief in Islam. If somebody believes in those principles, but because of some errors does not believe in Islamic rules, that person is a Muslim, on the condition that disbelief in rules does not result in denial of the prophetic principle. . . . Fairness

requires that we do not accept the claim that Islam consists of accepting every rule and opinion offered by the prophet and the refusal to accept any of them, for any reason is tantamount to apostasy.

The founder of the Islamic Republic, who is a traditionalist theologian, posits that even denying the obligatory nature of daily prayer or pilgrimage (*hadj*), both of which fall under the theological category dealing with prayer and are accepted by all theologians, is not in itself apostasy. If such an argument can be made about rules dealing with these fundamental components of Islam, it can certainly be extended to rules that discriminate against women. Even in the context of traditional Islamic theology, then, there is room to reject laws that hurt women.

Third, over the past century reformist religious movements have tried to find new interpretations of religion, within the context of religious logic, that are compatible with modern rationality and human rights. Theologians have used several methods for correcting laws that discriminate against women.

The first is grounded in what can be called the "conservative critique." Many traditionalists argue that the Islamic legal system for women is essentially just but that some aspects need correcting to reflect our times. Their style is a form of mending; they resist change for as long as possible, and when resistance becomes too difficult or costly, they offer a limited solution to a specific problem. They invariably try to legitimize these changes by citing some Qur'anic verse or hadith; they address only specific problems and avoid a systematic approach. Regarding the right of women to divorce, for example, they suggest that a woman can, upon marriage, demand that her husband grant her the right to divorce. In such cases the woman's legal status is no doubt improved. But the fundamental principle—that divorce is the right of men and can be granted only when men give their consent—remains unchanged.

The second approach can be called the "historical critique." In this critique, we must place religious rules in their specific cultural and historical context to evaluate them. We know that a majority of Islamic rules, as enumerated in the Qur'an and in hadith, existed in Arabia before the advent of Islam. Islamic Shari'ah merely gave them a seal of approval. They call these "reconfirmed" rules (*emzai*). Only a handful of rules were formulated during the life of the prophet on the basis of Islamic ideas. These are called "foundational" rules (*ta-sisi*). Both reconfirmed and foundational rules (particularly those dealing with contracts) were based on economic and intellectual exigencies in Arabia in the time of Islam's founder. Some argue that if the historical circumstances have changed, the rules they gave rise to have become obsolete. For example, today no one thinks that the rules endorsing slavery are still valid. The same argument has been made about polygamy. According to some theologians, polygamy was practiced by tribal societies in which men were responsible for the safety of women and children. Today, when civic institutions can provide the protection needed by women and children, they argue, polygamy is unjustifiable. If we expand this point of view, we arrive at an important principle: that religious rules are applicable only to the time of the prophet, unless their usefulness in other times can be rationally established.

A third approach, which can be called a "radical critique," is more innovative and different in two ways. It is also more prevalent among religious intellectuals. Some argue that the Qur'an, as revelation, has a transhistorical and transcultural essence that speaks to all humans, at all times, and in all cultures; it also has a contingent or historical aspect that is a reflection of Arab culture at the time the book was revealed to the prophet. The prophet was forced to take into account the culture of those directly receiving his revelation in order to make his message more palatable to them, but the way the Arabs lived fourteen hundred years ago should not be privileged religiously over the values and social practices of other societies. Being a Muslim means accepting the essence, and not the historical aspects, of the religion. This interpretation holds that many religious rules (particularly those dealing with contracts) are simply contingent aspects of faith. Being a Muslim in no way requires belief in or dedication to these rules. According to these religious thinkers, the prophet simply used the Arab culture of his time as an example to demonstrate to future generations how they could give a society a more divine direction without tearing it asunder. This analysis suggests that all religious rules regarding women are contingent aspects of religion. Negating them in no way implies a rejection of religion or opposition to the prophet.

These are three positions some people of faith offer. The issues are different for secular thinkers. For them religion is nothing more than the history of religion, which is a history of discrimination and inequalities among Muslims and non-Muslims, men and women, slaves and freemen, clerics and non-clerics. When theology is politicized, and when the state becomes religious, these inequalities are forced on society by the religious state. For the secular, problems that are founded on religion, such as gender apartheid, cannot be solved by a different reading of religion. The solution is to separate the institution of the mosque from the state.

Most secular intellectuals see Iran's gender apartheid as an integral part of the country's general system of apartheid. Iranian apartheid is based on a particular interpretation of Islam that divides society into "insiders" and "outsiders." The class of insiders includes the coterie of the ruling Court, but extends beyond that to encompass all of the pious. This pervasive privileging of the rulers' ideology ends up creating gender apartheid, because every time the rulers increase inequalities between men and women, they receive the approbation of the traditionalists. The rulers have on occasion shown some flexibility and have even made some adaptations in their ruling ideology. And they have no qualms about suspending beliefs considered foundational to the faith, such as the sanctity of the mosque; the country's former Supreme Leader, Ayatollah Khomeini, once temporarily suspended belief in the oneness of Allah. But they have never wavered in their belief in the natural superiority of men over women, and its concomitant idea that women are less capable than men of using reason and bearing responsibility.

As secular intellectuals have emphasized, the ruling ideology conceives of society as analogous to a family, whose members are uninformed minors in need of supervision. This notion of guardianship is intimately connected to the traditional belief in Islamic jurisprudence, which maintains that among minors, women are the most minor of all, that among the uninformed, women are the most uninformed of all.

Many secular intellectuals believe that devaluing and humiliating women is not only in itself despicable, but that it also degrades the entire society. Their insight sheds light on many events in the history of the Islamic Republic. Every time the rulers want to intimidate their opponents, they increase their attacks on women. Their suppression of women today in fact signals their weakness. Seeking to bring the society around to their vision, they are being defeated by the condemnation they have received both externally and internally.

Leftist thinkers have paid special attention to the double exploitation of working-class women. Some secular theories assert that men in society try to conceal their own humiliation, or compensate for it, by showing off their power over women. The official ideology in Iranian society betrays a male inferiority complex that is unleashed on women. A litany of humiliations contributes to this inferiority complex, including the one resulting from historical backwardness compared with the West.

In the secular intellectuals' approach to the question of women, cultural critique is central. They point out that humiliating and insulting women, viewing them as sexual objects, and subjecting them to policies that institutionalize these views have contributed to the deterioration of men's attitude toward women. Iranian culture, they say, has regressed much in this area since the advent of the Islamic Republic. Criticism of women's subjugation, they stress, must not be confined to politics and law. Rather, fundamental cultural change is needed: a democratic re-education of the entire society, which requires imbuing men with the spirit of freedom and equality.

When we talk of secular intellectuals, we must bear in mind that not all of them are anti-religion, although they accuse religious intellectuals of a vain search for modern progressive ideas in religion. It is possible to have faith, even Islamic faith, and yet believe in secularism, in the separation of church and state, and in the potential of reason to assess and explicate the affairs of this world. In the West, there are many thinkers who hold religious beliefs but are secular in their approach and offer radical critiques of the religious tradition. According to some who are indebted to feminist critiques of patriarchy, traditional religion has been formed by masculine sensibility and cognition. In the age of the Enlightenment, Kant warded off those who saw religion as mere superstition by insisting that religion remain in the realm of reason. Feminist critics today rightly point out that Kant's reason still had obvious masculine qualities and that modern religion must embrace the kind of sensitivity and cognition that invites all to peace and coexistence. Peace is not possible without equality between genders. Rejecting ideas that lead to gender apartheid is the primary mark of a humanitarian and ethical society.

What can be done to fight gender apartheid? We must begin on three fronts: culture, law, and politics. But we need to work on culture more than anything else. Discriminatory laws against women have their genesis in traditional images of men and women, in ideas about "femininity" and "masculinity." As long as these images pervade our society and family lives, the status of women will not improve much. These images have deep roots in religious as well as non-religious literature, so our first task is to become conscious of them and subject them to criticism. In my view, we must recognize that the following deeply embedded, traditional views on gender are not "natural":

Boys and girls do not have the same ability to master technology. According to this view, women do not have sufficient rational and logical faculties, and tend to be more emotional and instinctive. In traditional literature, women are symbols of the soul, while men represent reason;

Differences in body, mind, and psyche should dictate men's and women's roles in society and family; therefore, it is natural that men take the lead in these social hierarchies, since a healthy society is like a healthy body, and in a healthy body, the mind dominates the passions;

"Justice," according to our ancestors, is putting everything in its natural place. Thus, if women's natural place is to be subservient to men, then men's domination over women is a requirement of justice;

Boys should be raised for roles that

are natural to their capacities (like management, supervision, and leadership) and girls for naturally feminine roles (like bearing children, housekeeping, and taking orders). The poet Sa'edi describes the "ideal good woman" as one who obeys her husband's orders, keeps herself for her husband, and has, as the ultimate goal of her life, making her husband, and not herself, the "king." The good, obedient, and pious woman turns a poor man into a king;

Since in the traditional vision women are naturally inferior to men, they cannot enjoy equal rights with them;

Any change in the "natural" order can only bring about ruinous consequences for everyone, including women.

Given these deeply entrenched, mutually reinforcing ideas about gender, we must begin our cultural effort in the household, in schools, in our textbooks and our pedagogy, and in the way we raise our children. In the context of the family, we must recognize that in the nature of familial relationships and division of labor, injustices hurt women. Assigning social roles and responsibilities can be considered just only when men and women are afforded an equal chance to take them on; when they accept roles commensurate with their individual abilities and talents; and when their choices are made freely. Otherwise, the structure of the family and of society will remain unjust. I am not suggesting that traditional roles for women in the household and society are unjust. But it is unjust to force these roles on women.

In families founded on women's degradation and humiliation, it is difficult to raise sons who respect women. It is also hard to raise daughters who believe in their equality with men and have the self-confidence and independence they need to compete with men in the social arena. As a corrective, both mothers and fathers should perform roles traditionally regarded as masculine or feminine. Men must spend more time with their children and women must take more active roles in activities outside the home. This process will heighten our children's awareness of the gender inequalities around them, and will help us raise children who find gender apartheid as despicable as political apartheid.

There is a second important point I would like to make about Iranian culture and family life. This relates to our idea of the morally good human being. We all strive to raise good and laudable children. We generally do this with a conscious or unconscious image of the "good person." Unfortunately this image is invariably masculine or male-centered, synonymous with the "good man." For example, we refer to a solid and dependable promise as a "manly promise," and when someone shows compassion and justice, we say that that person has behaved in a manly manner. The Arabic word for compassion, *morrova*, has at its etymological root the word *mor*, which means manly.

If we look at the list of characteristics that our mystics have considered "masculine" and "feminine," we notice that most of the qualities we consider virtues are associated with men. According to stereotype, men are independent, competitive, aggressive, forceful, rational, inattentive to appearances, dependable and reliable, sexually active, and inarticulate about emotions.

Women are dependent, cooperative, emotional, sensual, tender and nonviolent, overly concerned with appearances, disciplined and tidy, in need of protection, sexually passive, and comfortable articulating their feelings. But we must define moral virtue and vice independently of gender. If independence is a virtue, it is a virtue for both men and women. If the spirit of cooperation is a virtue, it must be a virtue for both genders. That is why parents must, within the confines of family life, teach their daughters to become independent and self-reliant, to follow logic and reason, and to show firmness when necessary. They must also teach their sons to cooperate, and to articulate their emotions without shame. The goal of families, in short, must not be raising good men or women but good people.

Rethinking traditional notions of masculinity is also a great challenge on the legal front. Legislators made these discriminatory laws against women based on what they assumed were lordly edicts. Some of the traditionalist theologians do not consider it necessary to garner public support for laws that are founded on Shari'ah. In their view, God's commandments must be implemented, regardless of public approval. More moderate theologians have suggested that since the majority of the people are religious, the rules of Shari'ah become law on account of the majority's desire, and respecting these laws becomes incumbent on every citizen. For example, covering women's bodies according to Islamic rules (*hejab*) becomes mandatory even for non-Muslim women.

But neither position holds up. Civil

laws cannot be deemed enforceable simply on religious grounds. And lawmakers
must never pass laws that conflict with
principles of human rights (including the
rights of the society's minorities).

Let me explain these two claims.
Assume, for example, that some people,
based on their religious beliefs, think that
following *hejab* should be mandatory for
all members of their society, and they require it by law. In such a case, the rights of
non-Muslims, or of Muslims who prefer
not to follow these dress rules, are violated.
Some might claim that following religious
rules, including *hejab*, will bring about
the health and spiritual salvation of a society, and that everyone, even nonbelievers,
who is forced to accept these rules will ul-
timately benefit from their consequences.
What if, however, the same people were

to move to another society where followers of another religion are in the majority, and this majority enforces their rules on the society at large? What if, for example, the second society forbids girls to cover their hair in public schools? Most likely followers of the first religion will object, claiming that the rule conflicts with freedom of religion and human rights. Their claim is certainly valid. But if the rules of the second society are unjust, so must be the first. This is, in fact, precisely what is happening today: in Iran, religious fundamentalists insist on enforcing Islamic rules of *hejab* on everyone. At the same time, when countries such as France attempt to bar girls from wearing Islamic *hejab* in public schools, the same fundamentalists suddenly become defenders of human rights and religious freedom. The double standard is untenable rationally and morally.

If respecting human rights and religious freedom is a good thing (and I certainly think it is), then in our own society we must afford the same rights to those who follow other religions, or hold different ideas and opinions. The state must recognize the right of women to choose their own dress (as well as other rights). Laws and public policies must be based not on religion but on society's collective secular reason.

An important conclusion follows from what I have said: we must not support any law or public policy that limits our lives and behavior, unless there are rational, secular arguments favoring such limits. I mean arguments whose validity does not require belief in God, or in certain religious rules, or in the views of certain religious authorities.

Everyone agrees that laws must abide by moral principles, particularly the principle of justice. Why should morality take precedence over religion in the law? The precedence of moral principles over religion has in fact had many supporters among Islamic theologians both past and present. Most E'tezali theologians, who are rationalists indebted to Plato and Aristotle, and many Shia theologians have believed that moral principles (like justice) are defined independently of religion, take priority over religion, and even constitute the foundations for understanding and legitimizing religion. We must, in other words, first define the meaning and parameters of justice according to secular reasoning, and using that definition try to decide whether religion is just or not. Laws that breach human rights, including the laws that discriminate against women, are clear examples of injustice. Even the most devout must question their validity.

Defenders of women's rights must, along with their work in the cultural and legal domains, call for urgent and significant political action. We Iranians must fight for the concrete demand that the Islamic Republic join the Convention on the Elimination of All Forms of Discrimination against Women.

If the Islamic Republic signs this convention, it will commit itself to work toward seven clear goals: to include in its laws and its constitution the principle of equality between men and women; to pass laws prohibiting discrimination against women and establish penalties for such discrimination; to ensure the full implementation of these laws through the judiciary and other relevant institutions; to forbid public officials to discriminate against women; to use all means at its disposal to end any discrimination against women by any person, institution or organization; to eliminate all rules, regulations, and rituals that are discriminatory against women; and to repeal all discriminatory criminal laws.

Unfortunately, all attempts to urge Iran to join the convention have been blocked by traditional religious ayatollahs and fundamentalist groups. Among the top religious authorities, only one cleric, Ayatollah Montazeri, has supported this aim.

The women's freedom movement has a long, hard road ahead. But the horizon is bright as long as we do not forget that just laws and freedom can only come about through the efforts of women and men who prize these values. We must begin our work in our homes and schools. Our most important work is to raise children and citizens who love freedom and demand justice.

4

Islam and the West have had a long, complicated, and ambiguous relationship that has itself been subject to long, complicated, and ambiguous debate. Indeed, so overwhelming is the confusion that surrounds efforts to understand the relationship between Islam and the West that anyone in search of answers might be tempted to opt for silence.

Why has the relationship between Islam and the West been so vexed? The reason is that both sides have innumerable facets, and have had extensive interactions, often characterized by ignorance and confusion. My intention is merely to draw a broad map of this ongoing debate, which I hope will orient those interested in the possibility of easing tensions between Islam and the West. I offer here suggestions for how to begin a discussion. They will not end it. But I will start by offering four distinguishing aspects of Islam and the West, beginning with the West, in an attempt to illuminate their relationship.

The West is by and large Christian. For two reasons I did not say that the West is altogether Christian. First, other religions and faiths have long existed in the West, although their role has been minimal. Second, Christians in the West do not live the way they did during the dawn of Christianity, the age of the Church Fathers, or during the Middle Ages. Today the life of a Christian in the West is influenced by a number of new factors, including modernity. Secularism is one of the most important characteristics of the West, and while it has by no means eliminated Christianity from the public domain, it has certainly limited its influence. Nevertheless, most Westerners still define their identity in the context of Christianity.

The West was the birthplace of modernity. Even now that modernity has spread throughout the world, it remains deeper and more expansive in the West than anywhere else.

The West enjoys material superiority. I am referring to all material and external aspects of a society, including economic relations, production, distribution, consumption, agriculture, industry, transportation, and communication. Westerners enjoy a higher level of material welfare than people from other parts of the world. Military power has also played a crucial role in leveraging this superiority to dominance over other civilizations.

The West enjoys cultural and spiritual hegemony. Here, what I mean by culture is the totality of a society's spiritual and subjective aspects. Beliefs and perspectives, emotions and ideals, approaches to science and knowledge all fall under the rubric of culture. Many aspects of Western culture have proved desirable to those outside the West, and its desirability has helped it to achieve its cultural and spiritual hegemony. In my view, the most laudable Western innovations include the process of trial and error for arriving at the truth, as well as the principles of attention to reality (as opposed to dogmatism, prejudice, and superstition), rationalism (inimical to blind obedience and emulation), and egalitarianism (a foe of unjustified hierarchies). Another desirable aspect of the West is methodological and epistemological materialism, or the belief that every material phenomenon has a material cause. The West is also anti-traditionalist in that it refuses to afford legitimacy to anything simply because it has historically been accepted or practiced. Finally, the West respects, at least officially, human rights, liberalism, pluralism, tolerance, and democracy.

Now I shall address the characteristics of Islam.

Islam is a religion. Like other religions, Islam offers its followers a map of existence; a book of laws; and a balm for their psychological and spiritual pain.

Islam, like any other religion, considers these three components infallible.

Islam appeared before modernity. Islam retains many of the values of a traditional and pre-modern era, in particular prizing obedience to authority and faith. It thus accepts certain hierarchies and sees the hand of God everywhere; it does not traditionally accept free thought or pluralism.

Islam is currently in a defensive mode. For reasons too complex to detail here, Islam began its gradual decline in relation to the West at the time of the Renaissance when the golden age of Western civilization commenced. The decline accelerated when the world of Islam encountered the Western world in the eighteenth century. Napoleon's entry into Egypt in 1798 is arguably the most striking manifestation of this decline. Islam has been on the defensive since then, and has sometimes even nurtured a victim mentality. Today, in spite of a kind of awakening among Muslims globally and the rise of aggressive Islamic fundamentalism, the world of Islam remains in a defensive mode. In fact, the rise of fundamentalism and terrorism can be analyzed in the context of this defensive mode.

Lastly, Islam is polyphonic. There are various interpretations of Islam. Throughout the religion's history, the Islam of mystics has diverged from that of clergy, while the Islam of philosophers has offered yet another reading. After the initial cultural encounter between the Islamic and Western civilizations, this polyphony has become more pronounced. Among the wide varieties of interpretations today, three are most salient: modernist, fundamentalist, and traditionalist Islam.

Fundamentalist Islam subordinates the rational mind to the teachings of the Qur'an or the hadith (words or deeds attributed to the prophet Mohammed and his progeny.) Reason is valued only to the extent that it can mine the truth buried in these texts. Fundamentalist Islam emphasizes the superficial aspects of Islam to the detriment of its spirit. It considers religiosity to consist, more than anything else, in following the dictates of Shari'ah; moreover, it considers these dictates unchanging and beyond reproach. As a result, this version of Islam strives to establish a society in which Shari'ah dominates every aspect of life. This version of Islam does not accept religious pluralism; it considers Islam sufficient for satisfying all material and spiritual needs. It has animosity toward the modern West, which it views as against Islam, and against Shari'ah and *fegh*; it blames the West for the problems faced by the world of Islam.

Modernist Islam considers the rational mind a tool for finding the truth in the holy book and in hadith, but also for apprehending other sources of knowledge. It emphasizes the spirit of Islam rather than its appearances; it considers religiosity fundamentally a matter of living morally. It does not view the dictates of Shari'ah and *fegh* as infallible or unchanging, but believes that they are subject to the vicissitudes of time and place. According to modernist Islam, dogmatic insistence on these dictates causes estrangement from the eternal message of Islam; it has no interest in establishing a society wherein dictates of Shari'ah are implemented just as they were fourteen hundred years ago. Instead it endeavors to render these dictates compatible with human rights and universal morality. This version of Islam believes it is both possible and desirable to have a religious society in a secular political system. It endorses religious and political pluralism, and cherishes religion only as a source of solace for spiritual needs, not as a solution for material problems. Its adherents often defend Western civilization and culture on the grounds of its success in satisfying the material needs of its people. In their view, the greatest foes of the Islamic world are not foreign but local; the source of what has befallen us is in us.

Traditionalist Islam combines elements of fundamentalist and modernist Islam with its own unique aspects. Like fundamentalism it considers the rational mind only a tool for understanding the holy book and hadith, not for any other purpose. Its distinctive characteristic is an emphasis on intuitive gnosis. If it ever engages in hermeneutics, it is only through the use of the intuitive, not rational, mind. It does not embrace freedom of thought or shun dogmatism. It emphasizes the spirit of Islam and considers piety an internal voyage for which religious teachings are necessary but not sufficient. It doesn't consider Shari'ah and *fegh* as ends in themselves but simply as essential tools for a spiritual life. Traditionalist Islam is not preoccupied with establishing a society dominated by Shari'ah and *fegh* but focuses its energies on promoting morality and ethics. It is not dismayed by separation of religion and politics, and it believes in pluralism. Religion, in this reading, promises spiritual solace, but not earthly paradise. It is critical of the West and considers its culture a manifestation of human frailty. Yet it also considers Muslims, not Westerners or foreigners, responsible for the deplorable conditions of Islamic societies.

With this outline of the major characteristics of Islam and the West, we can make the following sketch of their relationship.

Because the West is by and large Christian, and because Islam is also a religion, the conflict between them is in part what one expects between any two world religions. There is opposition to Christian missionaries throughout the Muslim world; and Western countries have likewise placed some restrictions on the proselytizing activities of Shia, Sunni, or Wahhabi Islamic sects. Although the latter are not nearly as strong as the former, the difference owes more to Western countries' respect for freedom of religion and freedom of expression than to a Western embrace of Islam. The antagonism between Muslim and Christian theologians can also be characterized as the expected conflict between world religions. The growing number of Islamic and Christian theological treatises, written as apologia for their faiths, is another signal of the conflict.

If theologians of both faiths, however, consider that the fundamental conflict of our world today is between materialism and spirituality, they might overlook their differences and form a united front of those advocating spirituality. Unity between Christianity and Islam is particularly plausible because the Abrahamic religions in fact share a great deal. If theologians were to take as their models ecumenical thinkers like Thomas Merton and Hans Kung, they might work together to strengthen efforts to put people's non-material needs on a global agenda.

Islam and Christianity appeared before the advent of modernity and they face similar difficulties. Compared to Islam, however, Christianity has a less elaborate religious jurisprudence, and consequently has less difficulty coexisting with modernity; it can more easily accept pluralism and human rights. Islam, with its detailed jurisprudence, confronts many obstacles on this path. Nevertheless, it is clearly in their interests to cooperate in their efforts to reconcile religion and modernity. Both faiths should absorb into the culture of faith those aspects of modernity that do not conflict with the essence of religion— everything, for example, from modern conveniences to the right to vote. The aspects of modernity that do irredeemably contradict religion—like extreme individualism and materialism—should be weakened through the power of reasoned arguments, marshaled jointly by adherents of both faiths. Unfortunately, Islam is in a defensive mode, and invariably, societies and individuals in a defensive mode fall prey to paranoia, xenophobia, and rancor. Muslims are susceptible to the belief that Christian theologians aim only to weaken Islam and the Islamic world. Many Muslim theologians refuse to learn from the accomplishments of Christian theologians because they cannot tell friend from foe.

But Islam is polyphonic and its attitude toward Christianity and the West is likewise multi-faceted. Islamic traditionalists accept, even celebrate, Christian theology to the extent that it coincides with their own beliefs. The works of Rene Guenon, Frithjof Schuon, Titus Burckhardt, Martin Lings, Gai Eaton, and Seyyed Hussein Nasr are replete with Christian teachings, as well as extensive exegesis and defense of them. Many of these scholars, like Nasr, are themselves Muslim. Islamic modernists have drawn inspiration from modernist Christian theology. Indeed, in the last few decades, the work of Muslim modernists and traditionalists has contributed to softening the relationship between the Christian West and the Muslim world through finding common ground that exists in the spirit of both faiths. In the same period, however, Muslim fundamentalist clerics and Islamic ideologues have done everything in their power to undermine this relationship. Fundamentalist Islam's extensive jurisprudence, with teachings and rulings on all aspects of life, renders alliance with the West almost impossible, because the West exempts most aspects of culture from religious rules or puts them in direct conflict. Fundamentalist clerics have also completely rejected Christian theology and faith.

Yet Islam must face the difficult question of why it has suffered in the material domain and fallen so far behind Western civilization. Islamic theologians have responded in different ways. Some have argued that Islam was never intended to fix the material conditions of the world; its purpose is exclusively spiritual. Some fundamentalists believe further that divine intervention will bring apocalypse upon the West. Others have claimed that the West in fact used some Islamic cultural traditions—from commentaries on Aristotle to theories of astronomy by Muslim scholars like al-Biruni—to leave Muslims behind. And some scholars, such as Seyyed Hussein Nasr, have suggested that the West achieved a high level of material progress at the expense of its religious beliefs, and that Muslims were unwilling to give up their faith for it. But for those who believe that religions attend to the needs of both this world and the hereafter, this explanation doesn't convince.

Islam indeed faces a choice: it can adapt to the modern path of the West, or risk becoming increasingly weakened by its failure to address people's needs. Indonesia and Malaysia are too rare examples of the first choice. Only Muslim modernists are keen on understanding the West's progress and unlocking the mysteries of their own backwardness.

As Islam considers itself the supreme faith, it is further faced with the question of why the West enjoys such cultural and spiritual influence. Some, of course, deny its appeal, pointing to psychological and social problems rampant in modern Western societies. They even cite the fact that many Westerners are converting to Islam. Others have claimed that the West progressed culturally and spiritually only when it emulated tolerance for other faiths, and a spirit of inquisitiveness, in other words behavior that was in essence Islamic but appeared non-Islamic. A third group points to the cultural and spiritual appeal of the West as a sign of humanity's egotism, animal instincts and base behavior. Finally, another group considers the West's cultural popularity a sign of the end times.

Islamic modernists have accepted every virtue and accomplishment of Western culture and tried to incorporate them into the religious culture of Muslims. Islamic traditionalists have rejected Western culture, but they have never resorted to physical violence. Islamic fundamentalists have, however, in arguably the most brutal manner in Islam's history, employed violence, imprisonment, and torture to resist change. They view dissidents who show any inclination toward the West as the embodiment of evil, and inflict the cruelest punishments on them. The Taliban, Al Qaeda, and the Iranian clergy have all perpetrated these crimes. The Iranian clergy specifically perpetrated murder, attacks on bookstores and meetings, assaults on the clergy of other faiths, and the intimidation of students and dissidents.

Are there any conclusions to draw from this map that might help deescalate tensions between Islam and the West? In my view, the West must not use its material and civilizational dominance to consolidate its cultural hegemony. The values of Western culture exert sufficient appeal that the West need not use force to promote them. The West must cease using its military to advance Western expansionism in the Muslim world. Such acts only diminish the moral standing of the West. Democracy cannot be spread by bombs or missiles.

In dealing with the Muslim world, or other non-Western countries, the West must avoid policies that betray a double standard—for instance, ignoring Israel's nuclear bombs while insisting that Iran does not even have the right to enrich uranium for nuclear power. It is a legally indefensible position. Unconditional support for Israel coupled with indifference to the plight of the Palestinian people is another example. If despotism and oppression are bad, they must be considered bad everywhere.

The Islamic world must cease to define the West only through its conflict with Islam. Instead, the world of Islam must see itself as a partner in creating a new spiritual and moral world order.

Together Islam and the West must free themselves of the shackles of their historical memories. They must not allow their own future and the future of their children to be held hostage to a violent past. We must look to history only for lessons on building a better future, and we must forgo the temptation to use it to justify a new cycle of revenge and retribution.

With these foundations, there is hope for a peaceful coexistence, based on freedom, justice, and love. That is why I support liberal democratic humanism. The liberalism I believe in emphasizes freedom; the democracy I seek guarantees justice in the social, political, and civic realms; and the humanism I support advances global love, a love that transcends ethnic, national, racial, religious, and political lines. I support a republic of republics, which ensures democracy because it safeguards peace. It is well known that democracies do not fight one another. A democratic political system must be the goal of every country. When this is achieved a confederation of federal republics can be formed.

Religious and political fundamentalism poses the biggest obstacle to this ideal. Both the West and the Islamic world must use reason to reject fundamentalist readings of religion and politics. The role of the Islamic world in countering fundamentalism is crucial for achieving internal peace and harmony with the West.

The precondition for peace is tolerance, and the precondition for tolerance is that the pious of all faiths must accept religious pluralism and give up the conviction that their faith is superior. Today, Jewish, Christian, and Muslim fundamentalists all exploit the religious sentiments of the people only to promote war and the slaughter of the innocent. They must join forces instead and show that peace and the brotherhood of all faiths are the fundamental messages of Abrahamic religions. And they must also all strive to move religion away from the power of the state; they must demand the separation of church and state. The call of the Enlightenment and of Kant was this: Religion only within the confines of reason. Today, we can issue a new call: Religion only in the service of peace and friendship.

In his Sermon on the Mount, Christ said, "Blessed are the peacemakers, for they shall be called the children of God." (Mathew, 5:9)

BOSTON REVIEW BOOKS

Boston Review Books are accessible, short books that take ideas seriously. They are animated by hope, committed to equality, and convinced that the imagination eludes political categories. The editors aim to establish a public space in which people can loosen the hold of conventional preconceptions and start to reason together across the lines others are so busily drawing.